ISBN 978-1-4584-0429-9

HAL•LEONARD®
CORPORATION
7777 W. BLUEMOUND RD. P.O. BOX 13819 MILWAUKEE, WI 53213

BRIGHT LIGHTS BIGGER CITY

Words and Music by THOMAS CALLAWAY,
BEN ALLEN and TONY REYES

* *Recorded a half step higher.*

FORGET YOU

Words and Music by BRUNO MARS,
ARI LEVINE, PHILIP LAWRENCE,
THOMAS CALLAWAY and BRODY BROWN

WILDFLOWER

Words and Music by THOMAS CALLAWAY
and FRASER SMITH

Rubato feel

Who should I be? Wheth-er I'm _____ good or bad, ___ should lead us

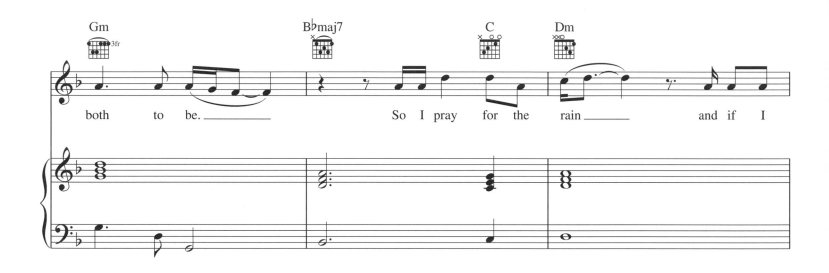

both to be. _____ So I pray for the rain _____ and if I

had her ev-'ry day, I'd still praise her the same.

You are to all, but you'll on - ly have to be beau - ti - ful ___ in the be - hold - ers' eyes.

Hold her with both my ___ hands ___ and put her right on the ta - ble when I get her home.

Won - der - ful wild -

flow - er, ___ oh, ___ o - pen up, let me

see. Ooh, ___ sex - y is in

BODIES

Words and Music by THOMAS CALLAWAY
and SALAAM REMI

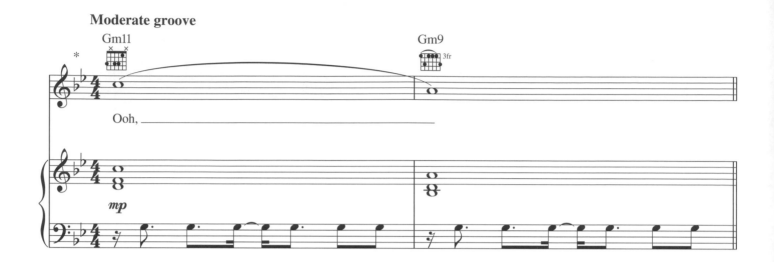

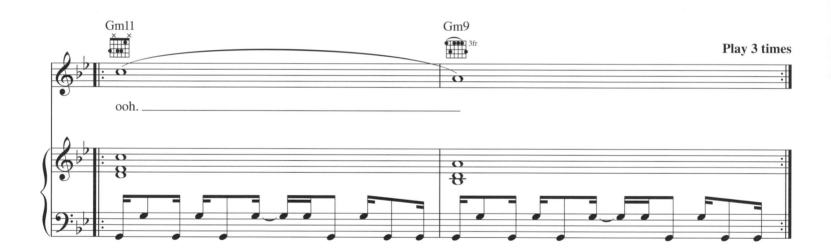

*Recorded a half step higher.

So by no means _____ was she in-no-cent. _____
Then I would face the time a mur-der-er gets. _____

(Spoken:) Well, it wasn't a crime if I didn't witness it.)
(Spoken:) Or get away with it. Life.

They said that chiv-al-ry is dead. _____

Then why is her bod-y _____ in my bed? _____

At sun-rise _____ the morn-in' pap-ers read, _____

they found a bod - y _____ in my bed, _

ahh. Ooh, _____
(Lead vocal ad lib.)

ooh. _____

Optional Ending

Repeat and Fade

Ooh, _____

LOVE GUN

Words and Music by THOMAS CALLAWAY,
MACK DAVID, JERRY LIVINGSTON
and TERRENCE SIMPKINS

SATISFIED

Words and Music by THOMAS CALLAWAY
and RICK NOWELS

Oh, let me sat - is - fy ____ you. ____

you. ____ Ooh, ____ I wan - na sat - is - fy

you, you, _____ you. ____

I wan - na sat - is - fy you, you, _____ you. ____

Ahh, _____ oh, let me sat - is - fy _____ you. _____ Let me sat - is - fy. _____

_____ you. Ahh, _____ the least I can do is try. _____

I want you to be uh, sat - is - fied. Ahh, _____ oh let me sat - is - fy _____

you. _____ Let me sat - is - fy _____ you.

Ahh, _____ the _____ you. Ahh. _____

I WANT YOU

Words and Music by THOMAS CALLAWAY,
FRASER SMITH and JACK SPLASH

Recorded a half step lower.

42

CRY BABY

Words and Music by THOMAS CALLAWAY
and RICK NOWELS

FOOL FOR YOU

Words and Music by THOMAS CALLAWAY
and JACK SPLASH

Slow groove

1. What, that real, that deep, that burn-in', that a-maz-in', un-con-di-tion-al, in-sep-'ra-ble love.
2. What, that deep, that sweet, that some-thin', that wet, that fire, that fall for stuff.
3. *Lead vocal ad lib.*

That feel like for-ev-er, that al-ways e-mo-tion-al but still ex-cep-tion-al love.
That up and that down, that front and that back, ba-by, I can't seem to get e-nough.

IT'S OK

Words and Music by THOMAS CALLAWAY,
HITESH CEON, KIM OFSTAD
and NOEL FISHER

Moderate Motown groove

Well, I wan-dered a - round_ af - ter our_ war of words_ and I'm wait-

OLD FASHIONED

Words and Music by THOMAS CALLAWAY
and ALAN KASIRYE

68

NO ONE'S GONNA LOVE YOU

Words and Music by BENJAMIN BRIDWELL,
CREIGHTON BARRETT and JAMES HAMPTON

70